cover TO cover

P

# 2 Peter

## LIVING IN THE LIGHT OF
## GOD'S PROMISES

**CWR**

Dave Edwins

# Contents

# Introduction

Born in 1948, Frank Abagnale, Jr. grew up in New York, but in his mid teens Abagnale embarked upon a life of deception that included bank fraud, posing as an airline pilot for Pan American World Airways (travelling over 1 million miles to 26 countries), posing as a chief resident paediatrician in Georgia and as a law student in Louisiana's State Attorney General's office. Eventually he was caught and imprisoned, but was later bailed by the FBI in order to assist their fraud prevention department. Still alive today, he has his own fraud prevention advisory company. Frank's story is told in the film *Catch Me If You Can* (2002), starring Leonardo DiCaprio and Tom Hanks. This true story seems so implausible – how could so many people be fooled?

In the second letter of Peter, the writer is eager to expose the first-century conmen who were duping young believers. Their arguments appeared believable, but spelt danger for the congregations of believers scattered around the Roman Empire.

There have been many discussions over the years amongst biblical scholars about the authorship of this little book of three chapters. Some believe it to have been written by an author other than Peter. Its similarities with Jude are cited as a reason for doubting its authorship and it was one of the last books to be admitted to the New Testament canon. However, there are many who do believe it to have been penned by Peter, or at least by his amanuensis or transcriber. The evidence for this view revolves around the writer's claim to be Peter and an apostle. In chapter 1, he declares that he was a witness to the transfiguration of Christ on the mountain. The use of the Old Testament scriptures would suggest that he was a Jew. It would seem that he was an old man and anticipating death (1:13–14). In the final chapter, the writer refers to a previous letter that he has written (3:1). Add to all of that the similarities of words used and some common teaching, and we may assume that this is indeed a genuine letter from Peter.

If 2 Peter was written soon after the first letter, then it would need to be dated in the mid sixties of the first century, as it seems likely that Peter died under the persecution of Emperor Nero. He was following up that first letter to the Christians who lived in the Northern parts of Asia Minor (what we recognise as Turkey today). Having warned them about the impending persecution that would sweep through the empire, the intention here is to warn his brothers and sisters about the dangers of false teachers. He wanted to encourage them to remain steadfast and be on their guard against those who would seek to lead them astray.

As Peter urges these believers to remain steady in their faith and doctrine, amidst the onslaught of heresy and false teaching, he emphasises the need to cling to a true knowledge of God. So throughout the letter you will find the word 'knowledge' repeated, in fact, at least fifteen times in the three chapters! However, when this word is used it is not to promote more 'head knowledge' but rather the knowledge that comes through a personal relationship with Jesus. Knowing Jesus in this way helps develop effective, godly living that will impact a watching world (1:3; 3:14,18). Peter further reminds his readers to stick close to God's Word – a great weapon in the spiritual battle to which they are called (1:4,19–21; 3:1–2,14–16). The alternative does not bear thinking about, as they would be giving ground to 'destructive heresies' (2:1–3).

So Peter issues a clarion call against false teaching and seeks to help his friends understand the harmful implications for accepting such teaching. Distinguishing between true and false doctrine would prove to be a tough task, especially as the source was from teachers who purported to be knowledgeable in the truth. So Peter warned his readers that they were to be on their guard and grow in their love and knowledge of Jesus (3:17–18) 'who is the way and the truth and the life' (John 14:6).

It is clear in this short letter that Peter is eager for his Christian brothers and sisters to keep growing in their faith and live in the light of the return of Christ. There is no uncertainty in Peter's mind that Christ would return (see chapter 3). It may be delayed but its immanence should stimulate our desire to live in ways that please Him. There is a call to live in holiness, diligence and in humility as the coming of Christ draws nearer (3:11–12). Yet even in the joy of welcoming Christ, Peter is mindful there would be sadness because His return would herald judgment for those who opposed the truth and led others astray (2:3).

The thrust of Peter's second letter is this: those who truly know Christ as their Saviour and Lord should live out their faith and grow in His grace and knowledge, in order that through their devotion to Christ, He would be honoured and made known to others around them.

WEEK 1

# Inheritors of God's Promises

## Opening Icebreaker

Think of a time when someone made a promise to you, which they then went on to keep faithfully (it may have happened recently or be from a childhood memory). How did it make you feel when they kept their promise?

## Bible Readings

- 2 Peter 1:1–4
- 1 Samuel 20:1–17
- 2 Samuel 9
- Romans 4:18–25
- Hebrews 10:19–23

## Opening Our Eyes

As with the first letter, Peter identifies himself as an apostle of Jesus Christ. Closer examination of the text shows that the writer was an eyewitness to the ministry of Jesus (1:16–18). There is no intention here of lording it over these young believers like some of the false teachers frequently did. In total contrast, Peter links his apostleship to servanthood – he claims to be a slave of Jesus Christ. To be a slave in the ancient world meant total possession by a master – to be no longer your own person, to have no personal rights and to be totally surrendered to your master's every whim. Peter happily relates this to his own position in Christ, he was content to serve his new Master, Jesus Christ, and live in obedience. He had given up his rights in order to serve the King of kings.

Much of the letter is taken up with describing what authentic Christian living looks like, because before you can detect the counterfeit, you must know the truth (like bank clerks who spend much time examining authentic currency in order that they may recognise forgeries).

Like other New Testament writers, Peter stresses the importance of faith in Jesus Christ. Their faith, he declares, is no different to that of the apostles and leaders and is just the same for us today. There are no super-saints in the economy of God, only those who have trusted in the saving work of Christ.

There seem to be three important dimensions to that faith, which are drawn to our attention. Firstly, it is all wrapped up in the person of Jesus and Peter heralds the fact that Jesus is God. He is not making a distinction between God the Father and Jesus the Saviour (v1), but rather declaring that Jesus is both Saviour and God (see also Titus 2:10,13; 3:4). As Saviour, Jesus brought deliverance from sin through His death on the cross, setting believers free from the tyranny of Satan so that now we can be recipients of His grace, righteousness and love. We can never earn righteousness or a right standing with God, we can only receive it by faith.

Secondly, this work of salvation can only be completed in us by the power of God (v3). Peter makes it clear that living a life of godliness is impossible for us to achieve without the divine power of Jesus. This power is available to us right from the moment we were born into the family of God and yet how many of us live unaware of God's great resources? The false teachers often offered supplementary knowledge as a key to living, whereas for Peter it is all wrapped up in the salvation package.

Thirdly, the reproduction of Christ's life in us can only be accomplished because of the certainty of God's promises. Knowing and believing His unchanging Word is crucial if we are going to develop a godly life. What an amazing statement that we 'may participate in the divine nature' (v4)!

Peter declares that we are alive because God puts His divine presence within us and we display godliness because of the certainty of God's power and promises. How good it is to know that we can tap into the resources of heaven and therefore be assured of God's faithfulness. As recipients of the divine nature, we should have a desire to live in a godly way, demonstrated in every area of our lives.

## Discussion Starters

**1.** What word, phrase or sentence stood out for you as you read 2 Peter 1:1–4?

_____

_____

_____

_____

**2.** How important do you think it was for Peter to identify himself as a servant? This concept is sometimes used in secular leadership context, but how important is it for the Church?

_____

_____

_____

_____

**3.** Peter talks about receiving faith (v1). Share or write down your story of how you came to faith and spend time thanking God for His grace.

_____

_____

_____

_____

**4.** There is mention of the 'knowledge of God' (v2), but this is not the human learning or intelligence that Paul condemns in 1 Corinthians 1:18–2:5. Tease out what you think is being referred to here.

_____

_____

_____

_____

**5.** It is impossible to live a holy life pleasing to God without the power of the Holy Spirit. What are the implications of this statement for you (see v3)?

_____

_____

_____

_____

**6.** Peter calls upon us to 'participate in the divine nature' (v4). What will this look like in our family, work or church lives? How can we help each other to live in this way?

_____

_____

_____

_____

**7.** It is all too easy to see the evil practices that surround your community, but what is God prompting you to do to bring light into the darkness? How can you demonstrate Jesus right where you are?

_____

_____

_____

_____

**8.** Most of the New Testament letters are liberal in their use of the word 'grace' (v2). What does this lovely word mean to you and why is at the heart of the good news of Jesus?

_____

_____

_____

_____

## Personal Application

Trace the development of Peter's thinking in these verses – faith in Jesus leads to us experiencing an overflowing measure of grace and peace. This is accomplished by the power of the Holy Spirit at work within us and we enjoy the delight of knowing that we have been called to follow and serve Him. As we grow in the love and knowledge of our Saviour Jesus we start to enjoy the delight of His precious promises. People looking on will be aware that we are different and that something of His family likeness shines through our daily living. Spend some time doing a spiritual checkup and perhaps challenge yourself about how much you have grown in your faith this year.

## Seeing Jesus in the Scriptures

Peter's life was transformed by the meeting with Jesus beside the Lake of Galilee. His journey since that time had not been easy and although there had been many highlights, there were also the beatings and the imprisonment. Even as he wrote this letter there was the likelihood of execution by Nero, who seemed determined to eradicate Christians from Rome. Yet in spite of all of that, Peter drew strength from a living Lord who having called him to Himself, would graciously fulfil His promises and transform Peter into His own likeness. Peter is now intent on setting Jesus centre stage so that in the light of the One who is the truth, the inconsistencies peddled by false teachers would be shown up as lies and deceit.

Here, there is a call to grow in the love and knowledge of Jesus so that we might be those who share in His risen life.

WEEK 2

# The Power of His Promises

## Opening Icebreaker

Think about someone who has profoundly influenced your life for good. It could be a teacher or maybe a church leader. What was evident in their lives that made a difference to you? How could you be a positive influence on those younger in the faith? (The list of qualities in 2 Peter 1:5–7 might help.)

## Bible Readings

- 2 Peter 1:5–11
- Romans 4:16–25
- Romans 5:1–5
- Galatians 5:16–26
- 1 John 1:5–10

## Opening Our Eyes

In the light of all that Peter has written in the previous verses, he now calls upon his Christian friends to build on the foundation of their faith. The encouragement that Peter brings here is not to sit around expecting God to do it all for them, but rather to make an effort to develop Christian virtues in combination with His strength working in them. It has echoes of Philippians 2:12–13, where Paul urged the Philippians to work out what God had worked in. Faith must be accompanied by action or it is 'dead' (James 2:17). This is not an invitation to earn our salvation by works but rather to counteract passivity or laziness.

The list of seven virtues that are mentioned here (vv5–11) is not in any sort of order or hierarchy, but rather they each assist the common development. 'Goodness' in Greek can mean excellence or courage, so faith leads to good or excellent living that in turn is enabled by courage. Knowledge seems to mean wise discernment or knowledge of God's will. Mastery of self is always tough and many of us will struggle to keep a grip on ourselves. Perseverance comes from the lovely Greek word *hupomone*, which entails an active looking forward, not just endurance of the present. We see it worked out in Jesus (Heb. 12:2). God likeness or godliness involves the desire to be in deeper relationship with God in order that His life might shine through. Love for our fellow Christians and others is a key quality that should mark our faith. The concluding virtue, *agape* or self-giving love, sums up the rest – a God likeness that is shown in the way we self sacrifice in order to bless others and is at the very heart of the mission of Jesus.

The characteristics that Peter calls us to display are crucial if we are truly going to be effective followers of Jesus. A lack in this area will make us fruitless and unproductive in our walk with Him. There is a contrast drawn here with those who are following false teaching and displaying a blindness and short-sightedness. Those who are following the upward way should be walking in light and not shutting their eyes to the needs around them. How easy it is to become insulated from the desperate needs around us. Take off your blinkers, Peter pleads! Christ's amazing work of grace has dealt with our past sinful behaviour and brought cleansing.

There is no need to be hung up on the final words of this section, namely election and calling. Suffice to say, if we have responded to the good news of Jesus, we have done so because God has called us by His Spirit and therefore we are part of His elect. The Greeks often used the phrase 'abundant entrance' or 'rich welcome' to describe the homecoming of a winner in the Olympics. When Jesus returns or when we are called into His eternal kingdom, what a rich and lavish welcome awaits those who belong to Christ!

## Discussion Starters

1. Looking at the list of virtues Peter gives in verses 5–7, in which areas would you like to grow?

   _____

   _____

   _____

   _____

2. What could be wrong with the often-used phrase 'Let go and let God', especially in regard to discipleship?

   _____

   _____

   _____

   _____

3. What does an effective and productive Christian life or church look like? What changes might you need to make in your life in order to be more productive?

   _____

   _____

   _____

   _____

4. Think about your own faith story in the light of 2 Peter 1:9. As you reflect, write down the things you are thankful for.

   _____

   _____

   _____

   _____

**5.** We all have blind spots in our lives, so how can we help each other and point out problems without causing harm? (Psa. 139:23–24; 141:5 may help.)

_____

_____

_____

_____

**6.** How important is it to know that you are adopted into the family of God by His choice?

_____

_____

_____

_____

**7.** What are you particularly looking forward to when you meet the Lord? Are you prepared for His call or His return in glory?

_____

_____

_____

_____

**8.** Imagine the welcome that God has planned for you. Share with your group what you envision, or write it down.

_____

_____

_____

_____

## Personal Application

In total contrast to the behaviour of those who followed false teaching, Peter here urges his friends to make progress in their Christian character. There is no hint here that he expected transformation to just happen, but that they should be engaged in the process with God. How are you going to develop in the virtues that Peter writes about? Keeping a journal can help us to chart our progress on the Christian journey. If you already keep one, look back and remind yourself of how you have grown in the last six months. If this would be a helpful discipline, find a notebook and record your thoughts and prayers regularly. Asking 'What is God teaching me today?' is a good question to begin with. Then, 'What practical action do I need to take as a result?'

## Seeing Jesus in the Scriptures

It is so easy to lose perspective when things do not go as we had hoped or planned. Here in this passage we are exhorted to remember where we have come from and look forward in eager anticipation to what God has planned for us in the future. Jesus came to earth to bring us the hope of forgiveness and a new life. He will be there to welcome us into His heavenly kingdom. When we wholeheartedly believe this promise, we can face our present problems and difficulties knowing that they will not last – but an eternity with our Father in paradise will.

WEEK 3

# Jesus is the Promised One

## Opening Icebreaker

Collect together about twenty different objects and place them on a tray. Put the tray in the centre of the room and give the group a minute to observe what is on it (no making notes!). Cover the tray and supply everyone with a piece of paper and a pencil. Invite them to write down all the objects that they can remember in two minutes. Who can remember the most?

## Bible Readings

- 2 Peter 1:12–21
- Isaiah 7:14; 9:2–7
- Matthew 17:1–13
- Luke 2:22–38
- Acts 13:22–24

**Opening Our Eyes**

As memory has the tendency to fade over time, it is good to be reminded of the important truths of the good news about Jesus. Peter calls the attention of his friends to the fact that they needed to stay rooted in the truth revealed in Jesus. In verses 12–15 he uses words like, 'remind you', 'refresh your memory' and 'remember these things', in an effort to bring them back to the importance of apostolic teaching. False teachers were intent on influencing these people, whilst having no regard for the truth. So Peter encouraged them to look back to what it means to be in Christ and live in tune with Him.[1]

There is an interesting personal anecdote in these verses. Peter implies in verses 13–14 that he believes that his death is imminent and that he has prepared for moving home to life in the heavenly realm. The picture he uses is of packing up a tent in preparation for a journey, which would be a familiar experience for first-century Christians. He is perhaps reminded of the words spoken to him by Jesus in John 21:18–19. It is likely that Emperor Nero, who hated and feared Christians, had Peter killed during his savage persecution, but it did not take the apostle by surprise.

There were two powerful witnesses that Peter called upon for assistance as he sought to combat the insidious deception of the heretics. Firstly, he remembers the time that he, John and James were with Jesus on a mountain and they saw a glimpse of the glory of Jesus. We often refer to it as the transfiguration. Peter remembers the vision they saw and the voice they heard declaring the authenticity of Jesus as the Son of God. It was for him, it seems, not just a foretaste of the resurrection but of the glorious return of Jesus. Notice that the Gospels of Matthew, Mark and Luke record this incident as taking place just after Jesus taught His disciples about His return in glory. It is interesting that the Greek word for 'eye-witnesses' (v16), carried the meaning of not just standing by as observers but being participants in the unfolding drama.

Secondly, the ancient prophecies pointed towards a day when darkness would be vanquished and Jesus, the 'Morning Star' would appear (see Rev. 22:16). It is significant to see here, the importance Peter places on the authenticity of the Old Testament prophecies. These prophets did not speak out words that boosted their own importance but rather spoke as directed by God. Divine inspiration of Scripture is upheld and rather than these people speaking as mere mechanical robots, they were carried along by God's Spirit. The picture is of a sailing boat propelled by the wind and influenced in its direction by the power of the breeze.

It seems evident that the false teachers were claiming that their words carried divine approval and they had little regard for talk of the return of Christ. For them the delay in His appearing obviously meant that He was not going to return! The Early Church leaders understood the importance of prophecy, but it had to be tested (see 1 Thess. 5:19–21) and allowed, in order to build up the Church (see 1 Cor. 14:3). God still speaks today, through Scripture, preaching and in dreams, visions and pictures. What is He saying to you?

## Discussion Starters

1. Think back to your first encounter with the Bible. What verses impacted you most and can you still recite a favourite verse?

   _____

   _____

   _____

   _____

2. Peter had thought about some of the implications for the Church if he was to die. How can we prepare for the future?

   _____

   _____

   _____

   _____

3. What were the things that stuck in Peter's memory from the transfiguration (see vv16–18)? How important are they for us today?

   _____

   _____

   _____

   _____

4. Peter and his friends glimpsed something of the majesty and glory of Jesus on the mountain. How would you react if God met you in a similar way?

   _____

   _____

   _____

   _____

**5.** Read some of the prophecies concerning the coming of Christ (Isa. 7:14; 9:2–7; Micah 5:2; Jer. 23:5–6). How much do you think the prophets knew when they spoke these words?

_____

_____

_____

_____

**6.** How can we follow Paul's instructions on prophecy in 1 Thessalonians 5:19–21? Can you remember a time when you were helped by a 'word' brought in your church?

_____

_____

_____

_____

**7.** Why is the doctrine of the second coming so important for us as believers? Read 1 John 2:28 and consider what is being taught there.

_____

_____

_____

_____

**8.** When did you last meet with God in a dramatic or powerful way? Write down or share with your group what that meant to you and why it is important in your discipleship.

_____

_____

_____

_____

## Personal Application

Have you ever been on a course where you had to fill in an evaluation form at the end? Whether we enjoy participating in these or not, they are really important for the people running courses as they help to improve and add new ideas to their courses. It is all too easy in our spiritual lives to move quickly on to the next thing rather than remembering and evaluating. We need to remember that God is trying to teach us through the various situations of life and reflection time is important. One spiritual discipline that is so often overlooked is silence. Perhaps you can make some time in the next day or so to hit the pause button of your life and sit quietly in a comfortable place where God can speak to you. Look back over the lessons that God has been teaching you and ask Him to help you to listen better.

## Seeing Jesus in the Scriptures

Peter could look back to that incredible time on the mountain when he saw the Lord in all His glory. Those memories were really important to him as he faced the possibility of fairly imminent death. As you read the Bible, make it a standard practice to ask Jesus to reveal Himself in His Word. God speaks to us today in a variety of ways, perhaps through the beauty of His creation, maybe through a friend, listening to an explanation of His Word or through a worship song. Often He speaks through the most unlikely of circumstances and people. Always check whether what you hear resonates with the teaching of the Bible and is glorifying to Jesus.

### Notes
[1]William Barclay's excellent commentary draws our attention to the importance of remembering what we believe and being what we were called to be – W. Barclay *The Letters of James and Peter* (Louisville: Westminster John Knox Press, 2003)

WEEK 4

# The Dangers of Deceptive Promises

## Opening Icebreaker

If you have a few recent national newspapers to hand, look for stories that illustrate the problems caused by lies and deception. And/or think about a time when you have been gullible in a particular situation and share or write down what you have learnt from it.

## Bible Readings

- 2 Peter 2:1–11
- Genesis 12:10–20
- Joshua 9
- Proverbs 6:16–19
- 2 Corinthians 11:1–15
- 1 Thessalonians 2:3–5b

**Opening Our Eyes**

Throughout the history of Israel there had been many false prophets who had set out to lead the people astray. Elijah dealt with the prophets of Baal, and Jeremiah and Ezekiel also had to contend with those who preached an easy, popular and comfortable way (Jer. 6:14; Ezek. 13:16). In the first century, there was a breed of false teachers who harassed God's people. They acted like a fifth column within the church, purporting to teach the truth when in fact they were leading people off course. We cannot be sure who these people were but they do show remarkable similarity with the early Gnostics, who emphasised knowledge but were weak on character and ethical issues. One difficulty was that teachers were held in high regard and therefore those indulging in deceptive teaching were difficult to unmask. Peter was aware that there were considerable dangers for the Church if these deceivers were not exposed.

Notice the characteristics of the false teachers: firstly, they denied the Lordship of Christ. Many modern expressions of heresy will also flounder at this point. Secondly, they pursued lives of abandonment to sensual pleasure – they were 'depraved' (vv2,7). Thirdly they were greedy for monetary gain. Travelling teachers were often paid for their skills in teaching. Fourthly they were happy to use and abuse the ones that listened to them. They were manipulators who enjoyed the accolades given and the popularity that was afforded to them. Their interest was not in the sheep but in what they could gain through their position as teachers (see also 1 Tim. 6:3–5). The warning at the end of verse 3 is significant, suggesting that God is not asleep or unaware of their perversion of the truth!

In verses 4–8, Peter uses three examples of the way that God was not prepared to overlook evil. Angels that were caught up in Satan's fall from heaven were committed to imprisonment until the day of final judgment (perhaps these were the ones that Peter referred to in 1 Peter 3:19). The people of Noah's time who refused to listen to the warnings and accept God's offer of forgiveness are also mentioned. Finally, he draws attention to the inhabitants of Sodom and Gomorrah, who also did not escape the judgment of God. There was no doubt in Peter's mind that those who twisted the truth and refused to acknowledge the authority of God were in danger of falling into the hands of an all powerful and sovereign God. However, there is encouragement here for true believers, because Noah and seven other members of his family were saved from the destruction of the flood and angelic messengers rescued Lot, even if they did have to extract him against his will! We may be sure that our God does know how to take care of those who belong to Him.

These inexperienced believers were facing considerable challenges, for when basic doctrines are ignored or denied, an inevitable erosion of ethical standards ensues. The description accorded to these deceivers in verses 11–12 is revealing, as they are shown to be arrogant, blasphemous and slanderous towards church leaders. They had become like unreasoning animals whose destiny was destruction. Strong words from the apostle but are we in danger of being too tolerant when we face the power of evil in our world?

## Discussion Starters

1. How can we be on our guard against false teaching without being ungracious and suspicious? What is the role of church leaders in helping us deal with this?

2. What are the issues that mark a movement out as being a cult? Can you think of examples of where deviation has taken place and the resulting fallout?

3. Often money has been an issue for Christians. How can we ensure that we are generous and lavish in our giving?

4. How important do you think integrity is for the believer today? Are there ways that we can help each other to stay pure in terms of our ethical behaviour?

5. Power issues are often difficult for us to negotiate. Can you recognise any traits in your life that need addressing?

_____

_____

_____

_____

6. What is it about false teachers that make them so attractive? Look at the way the Early Church dealt with such people (1 Tim. 1:3–7; 6:3–5; Jude 17–23).

_____

_____

_____

_____

7. The subject of judgment is tricky for Christians especially in a tolerant age. How can we speak effectively of God's reckoning with evil and yet remain 'peddlers of grace'?

_____

_____

_____

_____

8. Has God ever had to rescue you from a trial? Share or write down stories of God's powerful grace at work in your life and turn it into a time of praise and worship.

_____

_____

_____

_____

## Personal Application

Under the three headings of money, sex and power do a check on your life as a Christian. Are there areas that God wants you to surrender, which would help you to be more effective in your witness for Him? Sometimes it is helpful to meet up with a friend who will hold you accountable and with whom you can be completely honest. Make a regular time for meeting and praying together. Work out a series of questions to ask and challenge each other with. You will find plenty of help on the internet and in books like *Soul Keeping* by John Ortberg.[1]

## Seeing Jesus in the Scriptures

The heretics, who Peter drew the attention of his young Christian friends to, had sadly departed from the truth about who Jesus was. Having spent much time in the company of Jesus whilst He walked the earth, Peter knew that Jesus was no ordinary man but in fact the Lord of glory. He had heard His teaching, observed the great miracles and seen people raised to life again. That made the plight of his friends even tougher for Peter to take and so he spelt out the dangers of departing from the truth of His sovereign Lord. The centrality of Jesus is fundamental to our faith and His incarnation, death and resurrection are the foundation stones under our feet. Make sure that you do not drift but remain firmly anchored to Him.

**Notes**
[1] J. Ortberg *Soul Keeping* (Grand Rapids: Zondervan, 2014)

WEEK 5

# The Destiny of Promise Deceivers

## Opening Icebreaker

If you are using this guide in a group, try the following game together. Write a few obscure biblical words on cards (five or six should be enough) and write the meaning below the word. Arrange for three people each time to give their version of what the word means, one of which must be the accurate description. The rest of the group has to guess who is bluffing and who is telling the truth.

## Bible Readings

- 2 Peter 2:12–22
- Numbers 22–23,25
- Galatians 5:16–26
- 1 Corinthians 2:1–8

## Opening Our Eyes

To the fisherman turned pastor, the sadness of the situation that beset his friends was intolerable. It seems that young and inexperienced believers were being led astray by deceptive promises made by those who had deviated from the truth found in Christ. They made offers of freedom that could never be realised because they only led to a dead end. The strange thing was that the ones involved in the deception were themselves in danger from the very things they were promoting. They were so arrogant that they even felt able to blaspheme and slander God's own name. They had at one time known Christ but now had turned their backs.

It is clear from this section that these apostates (ones that had renounced their faith) made a living out of leading people astray. Having deserted the foundation of their own faith they felt free to indulge in sinful conduct, with no thought of the consequences. The implication was that even the Lord's Supper or the love feast had been dishonoured by their adulterous activity. No one was safe from their desire for self-gratification and every young Christian was a potential target. In our own day too, we have observed the danger from the lust of sexual predators. Lives devastated by the delectations of older, more experienced and seemingly trusted public figures. Peter's holy anger here is but a mirror of God's hatred of this kind of abusive behaviour – predators baiting their hooks and reeling in the unsuspecting. In Greek, verse 14 suggests that these people had trained themselves deliberately for this perverted activity, as athletes would train for the games.

The illustration of Balaam is used by Peter to highlight the seduction of greed. The story, found in Numbers 22–23, shows a man who seemed to have prophetic insight from God, allow himself to be susceptible to financial inducement. The suggestion in 2 Peter is that his donkey had more spiritual understanding than he did! Then in Numbers 25 we read of God's people being led astray through sexual immorality, which was organised by the Moabites. So Balaam goes down in history as the one whose desire for financial gain, in turn, led God's people into sexual depravity. These were the very same temptations that confronted the believers in the first century, hence the example drawn.

The metaphorical description of these false teachers in verse 17 is powerful. They are like springs or water systems that have dried up, clouds promising rain but are driven away by the wind. They offer empty promises of freedom when they themselves are held in slavery. P.T. Forsyth is reputed to have said, 'The first duty of every soul is to find not its freedom but its Master.'[1]

The final verses of this chapter throw up some interesting thoughts. Is Peter suggesting that it is possible to lose one's salvation? It is perhaps more likely that these false teachers had not experienced the saving power of Christ and thus were not regarded as truly born again believers. If you compare the reciprocal passage in Jude 19, the writer declares these people to be without the Spirit of God, hence although they profess a sort of faith they could not be regarded as true believers (see Rom. 8:9).

## Discussion Starters

**1.** Peter described the false teachers as being bold and arrogant (2:10). What are the dangers of arrogance for the local church?

_____

_____

_____

_____

**2.** Blasphemy is fairly common in the world around us. Think of some examples that you have come across recently.

_____

_____

_____

_____

**3.** Living in a sexually orientated society, how do we stay pure in our thinking and acting?

_____

_____

_____

_____

**4.** What are the temptations regarding greed and materialism that threaten your walk with God? How do you manage to resist when the pressure is on?

_____

_____

_____

_____

**5.** The word 'freedom' is commonly used and abused in our society, but what is true Christian freedom? Consider again the quote from P.T. Forsyth.

_____
_____
_____
_____

**6.** Nelson Mandela once commented, 'For to be free is not merely to cast off one's chains, but to live in a way that respects and enhances the freedom of others.'[2] Discuss the importance of this for our discipleship. How are you enhancing the freedom of others you know?

_____
_____
_____
_____

**7.** Compare the passages in Hebrews 6:4–6; 10:26–31 and John 10:28. Do you believe it is possible to lose one's salvation?

_____
_____
_____
_____

**8.** How do we help and support our leaders so that they do not fall into the traps that the false teachers had? Discuss or write down the importance of accountability for all Christians.

_____
_____
_____
_____

## Personal Application

There is a call in this passage to live humbly and with holiness. This is a marked contrast to the demands of the present age in which we live. Faced with the seduction of false teachers, these young Christians were challenged by Peter to stay strong and live obediently to their Lord and Saviour. It is all too easy to become arrogant when you have found the certainty of the truth in Christ. Leaders have to constantly beware that they do not seek their own advancement and aggrandisement. Likewise, we all need to check ourselves for over confidence and conceit. The picture of Jesus in the New Testament is of a humble servant leader who calls us to die to self and live humbly pleasing God.

## Seeing Jesus in the Scriptures

Peter draws the contrast here between the arrogance and self-seeking desires of these enemies of the faith and the true humble, serving nature of Jesus. Knowing Him should encourage us to give a wide berth to greed. When we discover real faith in Jesus and commit to following His ways, we need to leave behind the old ways that were leading us on a path to judgment and destruction. Knowing Christ in a personal way brings forgiveness, a new direction and a new purpose for living. Only in Christ is true freedom found, and a way of escape from futile cravings of our own sinful hearts. The wonder of the incarnation and the power of the cross/resurrection are the truths that bring hope and transformation.

### Notes
[1]www.goodreads.com/quotes/692499
[2]www.anc.org.za/show.php?id=65

WEEK 6

# The Promise of Christ's Return

## Opening Icebreaker

Can you think of a time when someone scoffed at you for your faith? What did it feel like? How did you react? Try to unpack what it is that causes people to ridicule Christianity. Discuss or write down ways in which we can react positively and share faith effectively.

## Bible Readings

- 2 Peter 3:1–10
- Mark 13
- Philippians 3:20–4:1
- 1 Thessalonians 4:13–5:11
- Revelation 21

## Opening Our Eyes

Like any good teacher, Peter begins this section with reminders of previous teaching just as he had done in 1:12. Like these first century Christians, we too are prone to forget and, in the busyness of life, to become complacent about the important issues. So Peter calls their attention to the fact that the teaching he brings is compatible with apostolic teaching, Old Testament prophetic messages and the commands of the Master. It seems that the false teachers were sceptical and scoffing about the second coming of Christ. This doctrine is well rooted in the Bible. Prophets such as Isaiah, Jeremiah and Zechariah all made reference to the day of the Lord (see Isa. 2:10–22; Jer. 30:7; Zech. 14). Jesus is recorded in the first three Gospels as having taught about this before His death and resurrection. For the apostles it was a key theme of their preaching and writing (Acts 3:20–21; 17:30–31).

It seems highly likely that the reference Peter makes to a first letter (v1) is that of 1 Peter and not chapters one and two of this letter (or even a lost letter!) as some suggest. Certainly in 2 Peter 2 there is overlap with Jude, but perhaps both were drawing on a common source.

The emergence of teachers claiming that the second coming had already happened (or that it was never going to happen), was anticipated by Paul when he was writing to Timothy (2 Tim. 2:17–18). Throughout history there have always been cynics and sceptics who have dismissed the truth of God's promises. Noah met with opposition when he warned of an impending flood and Lot too found that his warnings were ignored in Genesis 19. There is an obvious reason why the second coming was scoffed at here: if you were living a life of debauchery and lustful arrogance then it was convenient to ignore and reject its reality. The very fact that Christ's return could happen at any moment is an excellent reason for living a life of holiness and expectation.

The argument that these teachers raised against the return of Christ revolved around the fact that they claimed nothing had changed in the functioning of the world since its creation. Therefore it was also highly unlikely that there would be any change in the future. Peter's response is that they seem to have forgotten that God is all powerful and that He created by His Word. Also, the flood during the time of Noah rather confounded their 'nothing ever changes' argument! These false teachers are further warned that God will judge evil, not with a flood but fire (v7), and they were in danger.

Some pointed to the delay in the return of Christ as evidence that God was not in control. This is countered by the assertion that the reason for delay is that God loves and is patient with His errant children. He dwells in eternity and therefore is not limited by time as we are. God has not forgotten but is exercising His love and mercy. The day would come but at a time totally unexpected as a thief in the night (see Luke 12:35–40 or read the parable of the foolish bridesmaids in Matt. 25:1–13). Some have related the words used by Peter to a nuclear explosion, with fire and noise. One thing is certain – God is in control of these events, not puny megalomaniac tyrants. So the call is to be watchful and prepared.

## Discussion Starters

1. Think about previous teaching you have received. Do you need to be reminded about something important that God has previously spoken into your life?

   _____

   _____

   _____

   _____

2. It is said that right belief leads to right behaviour. How can we motivate one another to 'wholesome thinking'? What are the dangers of unwholesome thinking?

   _____

   _____

   _____

   _____

3. What is the most common criticism of Christianity today? Discuss how you would answer a sceptic's questions with grace and truth. Try to discover what lies beneath the surface of a scoffer's response.[1]

   _____

   _____

   _____

   _____

4. The false teachers had a blatant disregard for God's Word and pursued their own deviations to justify their evil behaviour. How important is God's Word to you?

   _____

   _____

   _____

   _____

**5.** How does a strong belief in the second coming assist your discipleship journey?

_____

_____

_____

_____

**6.** What you are looking forward to most when Jesus returns? (If you have time, read Rev. 21.)

_____

_____

_____

_____

**7.** Are there some promises that you have received from God, which as yet have not been fulfilled? Pray about these things. Share or write down some of the great things God has given you, and give Him thanks.

_____

_____

_____

_____

**8.** In verses 9–10, we read something more of the heart of God. Are there friends and loved ones who you are praying for who have yet to respond in faith to Jesus? Name them and spend some time praying for them.

_____

_____

_____

_____

## Personal Application

What if you knew that Jesus was going to return tonight? How would that affect the way that you would live the next few hours? The problem for many of us is that we have become so used to thinking about Jesus' return in a future tense that we have lost the art of living constantly in the hope of His immediate return. I knew an old minister who would awaken each morning with this sentence on his lips, 'What if He returned today?' Take some time to examine your journey with God and think about what changes might need to be made in order for you to live constantly in the expectation of His return. I personally find 1 John 2:28 very challenging.

## Seeing Jesus in the Scriptures

The first Advent of Jesus was as a babe born to lowly parents living as refugees in Bethlehem. He came to our sin-sick world precisely because of the love of God for the human race, which had turned its back on Him. The nativity story demonstrates the amazing grace of God in practical terms. Luke records that after the birth of Jesus, He was taken to the Temple for circumcision and there He was welcomed by two old saints, Simeon and Anna, who had been waiting for the fulfilment of a promise given many years beforehand. They were confident that God always keeps His promises and their faith was rewarded. Peter reminds us that Jesus has promised to return and although we do not know the time or date, the promise is certain.

**Notes**
[1]For further reading: A. McGrath, *Bridge Building* (Nottingham: IVP, 1992)

WEEK 7

# Looking Forward

## Opening Icebreaker

In 1 Kings 3:3–15, God asked Solomon what he wanted most as a gift from heaven. Just imagine for a moment that God spoke to you in a dream and asked the same question. What would your response be? This could be a life changer, so share with the group or write down your request and dream.

## Bible Readings

- 2 Peter 3:11–18
- Genesis 12:1–9
- Genesis 37:1–11
- Nehemiah 1:1–2:5
- Acts 26:1–18

## Opening Our Eyes

In this final section of 2 Peter, a key word might be 'diligence'. The phrase 'make every effort' (3:14) appears to be important for Peter as he also repeated it three times in the first chapter (1:5,10,15). The Greek word *spoudazo* carries the meaning to hurry, to be bent upon, to strive or endeavour. One thing is certain, if we are going be successful on our Christian journey we have to play our part and not just coast along in neutral. It does take effort and the call of this letter is to be diligent.

The return of Christ in glory is a great motivator for holy living for the believer. As an older Christian once quipped, 'I have moved off the planning committee and joined the welcoming committee.'[1] Much has been written and argued over the years about how and when this event would occur, when it might be more profitable to prepare ourselves for that great day. The false teachers were so convinced that Christ was not going to return, they lived in almost complete abandonment to their sinful lusts. On the contrary, Peter instructs his friends to live holy and godly lives. Both these words are written in plural form, indicating perhaps there is no rigid narrow game plan for holiness but rather a grace-filled flexibility. Holiness can sadly so easily become a cold and rigid system of dos and don'ts.

Clearly Peter expected the return of Christ to bring judgment and an end of all things as we know them in our universe. The good news is that a new heaven and a new earth will replace that which has been destroyed. The emphasis upon fire suggests a purging of all evil as it is destroyed, making way for a home of true right living (v13). Notice the contrast between the true believers who are called to live spotless lives (v14), with the lives of the false teachers (2:13) who are full of blemishes. Perhaps this is a reference to the Jewish sacrificial system, which demanded an animal to be spotless and without defect (eg Exod. 29:1).

Notice the guarded way that Peter spoke of Paul, his fellow apostle, in verses 15–16. There were some who tried to make trouble between the two by stressing a supposed difference of doctrine. (It was more likely a difference of emphasis that the two apostles took.) Peter believed that the intellectual prowess of Paul occasionally led to problems in interpretation, which was exaggerated by false teachers.

There is a note of affection as Peter warmly sums up his writing to his 'dear friends' (v17). He urges them to be watchful and to distinguish between truth and error. Their enemies were subtle in their argument but nonetheless at heart were lawless, ungodly and corrupt in their behaviour. The analogy of the pigs (2:22) comes to mind here! Positively, Peter encourages his friends to keep growing in the grace and knowledge of the Lord. Transformation into the image of Jesus does not happen overnight and it demands that we diligently pursue a life of truth, guarding ourselves from false teaching and living an adventurous life full of dangerous wonder.[2] No doubt there would be trials and temptations ahead, almost certainly suffering as Roman persecution developed, but if they stayed close to their Master and allowed Him to live in them, He would be acclaimed and honoured.

## Discussion Starters

1. How can we honour Christ more in our daily living? Do our family, friends and neighbours realise that we are committed to following Him?

   _____
   _____
   _____
   _____

2. Referring to the return of Christ, how can we 'speed its coming' (v12)? (Read Mark 13, especially v10.)

   _____
   _____
   _____
   _____

3. What do you think our new earth and heaven will be like? Use your imagination based on biblical material. What will a 'home of righteousness' mean?

   _____
   _____
   _____
   _____

4. We've explored how a key word for Peter's letter might be 'diligent'. Would you describe yourself as a diligent Christian? What are the indications of being diligent in daily living?

   _____
   _____
   _____
   _____

**5.** Can you find examples of when God exercised patience with His people? These could be personal or for the nation of Israel.

_____

_____

_____

_____

**6.** Living in harmony is a tough call for sinful people. How are you doing in your church, fellowship and group? What are the things that destroy unity amongst God's people?

_____

_____

_____

_____

**7.** The Ephesian Christians seemed to be good at spotting heresy but not so good about deepening in their love (see Rev. 2:1–7). How is it possible to live on your guard against error without becoming paranoid and suspicious?

_____

_____

_____

_____

**8.** Are you growing in the grace and the knowledge of Jesus? Write down or share encouraging evidence of growth that you have observed in yourself or others.

_____

_____

_____

_____

## Personal Application

When it comes to talking about others, almost imperceptibly we can slip into gossip or even 'put down' mode. Peter could see there were some difficulties for people with Paul's amazing intellectual approach to theology (v16) and he acknowledges that but does not slip into attack mode. Rather, he shares his warmth towards Paul and strongly warns those who try to cause division to beware of God's judgment. How warm and generous are you towards those who you don't particularly agree with? How can you make space to discuss differences and develop greater harmony? Jesus instructed His disciples right at the end of His earthly life to remember that their love for one another would be a powerful witness for the good news (John 17:20–23).

## Seeing Jesus in the Scriptures

Throughout this short letter, Peter has constantly returned to the importance of the return of Christ. Our theology is sadly lacking if we do not hold tenaciously to this life-changing doctrine. If we lived day by day with this in view, what a difference it would make to our discipleship. It would inform and transform our conversations as well as our friendships. We may not know the date or even the full details of the manner of His return, but what a day to look forward to! We will see Jesus face to face and the battles with sinful behaviour that have dogged our footsteps will finally be over. Till that day let us grow in the grace and knowledge of our Lord Jesus Christ.

### Notes
[1] W. Wiersbe, *The Bible Expository Commentary Vol 2* (Colorado Springs: Cook, 1999) p466
[2] Further reading: M. Yaconelli, *Dangerous Wonder* (Colorado Springs: Nav Press, 1998)

# Leader's Notes

---

**Week 1:** Inheritors of God's Promises

### Opening Icebreaker

The idea of this exercise is to draw out the importance of promises and the keeping of them. Be aware that some in the group may find this conversation difficult because of broken promises in their lives. Concentrate on the positive examples but also pray for one another if talk of broken promises does arise.

### Aim of the Session

To begin to understand the importance of God's promises and to take to heart the faithfulness of God.

### Discussion Starters

**1.**   Give the group time to think about the passage and share something that emerges from the text. It is important not to rush this process. Make sure everyone has opportunity to share if they wish.

**2.**   We often talk about servant leadership but what does it mean in a Christian context? Is this an important value in your church or group? How can you encourage your leaders to be examples of this?

**3.**   This is an opportunity to share your faith journeys with each other. Concentrate on the difference between the before and after, and how people found Christ. Give the group a limited amount of time so that everyone who wants to share can be heard.

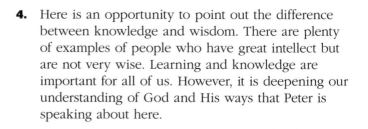

4.  Here is an opportunity to point out the difference between knowledge and wisdom. There are plenty of examples of people who have great intellect but are not very wise. Learning and knowledge are important for all of us. However, it is deepening our understanding of God and His ways that Peter is speaking about here.

5.  Discuss what holiness looks like in a twenty-first century context. Spend some time thinking about how vital the Holy Spirit is in our discipleship. Are we in danger of ignoring His essential work in our lives?

6.  The pagan thinkers of the day believed that humankind already had a share in 'divine nature', the problem was it was not evident in their daily living! Peter encourages these believers to live so close to Christ that His nature 'infused' them (see John 10:10).

7.  Discuss the areas of darkness in your local community. Consider what is already being done to address these issues (eg a food bank or volunteer initiative, like 'Street Angels') and think through ways that your group might partner with these. Maybe God is already envisioning you for something that is not being covered at the moment?

8.  Look at some of the outstanding examples of grace in the Bible (such as 2 Sam. 9 or Luke 23:39–43). How does grace work in our lives from day to day? Share an example of grace working in your life.

# Week 2: The Power of His Promises

## Opening Icebreaker

There have probably been people in your life like my old Sunday school teacher, Sam. He always believed in us and despite our unruliness at times, faithfully stuck to his task. What was it that made him so special? Work out what it takes to be an effective mentor, perhaps using the list in 1:5–7. Consider and pray about who you might mentor in the future. *Mentoring 101* by John Maxwell might help.[1]

## Aim of the Session

To focus on the building up of our faith by learning to depend on God's 'great and precious promises' (2 Pet. 1:4).

## Discussion Starters

**1.** You could also encourage each other with the following activity. Circulate pieces of paper, each headed with the name of a different group member, around the group so that everyone can write down something that they observe (area of strength) about each person. You could focus on the virtues stated in 2 Peter 1:5–7. Rotate the pieces in turn until they are returned to the person named on the paper. Then let everyone read their encouragements.

**2.** This phrase was in common use some years ago and seemed so spiritual to say. Talk about whether in fact that is what God expects from us or are we just opting out of our responsibility for our own discipleship?

**3.** Often we judge the effectiveness of a church by its numbers or number of programmes that it operates. Discuss what you think makes an effective church

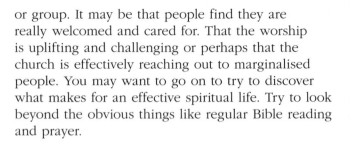

or group. It may be that people find they are really welcomed and cared for. That the worship is uplifting and challenging or perhaps that the church is effectively reaching out to marginalised people. You may want to go on to try to discover what makes for an effective spiritual life. Try to look beyond the obvious things like regular Bible reading and prayer.

4. This time do not share the actual story of your journey to faith but try to think about the significant events that have contributed to your growth in faith. For me, it was after failing my O-Level exams that I really began to ask God what He wanted to do with my life. For you it might be your baptism or confirmation, or other significant life events.

5. Think about significant times when a blind spot was exposed in your life. We often use the analogy of blindness to sight to represent a conversion experience. (Think about John Newton's famous hymn, *Amazing Grace*.) Is it possible that as Christians we too can be short-sighted or blind, as Peter suggests in 1:9? How can we help each other recognise a blind spot? How willing are we to be taught or challenged?

6. We sometimes shy away from words like 'election' and 'calling' (1:10). Read what Paul says in Ephesians 1 and try to tease out what is important for our growth. The fact that we know our salvation is not by human effort is comforting, for it reminds us that we are dependent upon an all-powerful and loving God.

7. What is so wonderful about meeting with God at the end of our earthly life? What will you miss about this life and what are you anticipating most? Larry Norman and Cliff Richard used to sing a song

entitled *I wish we'd all been ready*. Find the lyrics or listen to it on the internet.

**8.** If you can, find a copy of John Bunyan's *The Pilgrim's Progress* and read to the group an extract from the scene wherein Christian and Hopeful reach the Celestial City and enter the gates (the last section of Part I).

¹J.C. Maxwell, *Mentoring 101* (Nashville: Thomas Nelson, 2008)

---

# Week 3: Jesus is the Promised One

## Opening Icebreaker

The point of the game is simply to test memory.
A variation of the game is: after the group has observed the tray, take an item away (get everyone to close their eyes!) and then show the group the tray and ask them to guess what is missing. Once it has been guessed correctly, place the item back and take away a different item, again asking the group to guess what is missing. Repeat for as long as the group likes!

## Aim of the Session

To encourage us to never forget the great things God has done for us and remind us of the great truths of His Word, which have transformed our lives.

## Discussion Starters

**1.** Talk together about everyone's first encounter with the Bible, asking the following to help: When and why did you start to read the Bible? What did you think of it? What do you think of it now? Can you remember an early memory verse that you learned? What verse

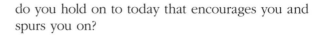

do you hold on to today that encourages you and spurs you on?

**2.** Peter seemed to know that his time on earth was coming to an end (1:15). Perhaps it was the gathering clouds of Roman persecution or maybe failing health. Either way he wanted to prepare his Christian family for that time and appears to be setting his affairs in order. How prepared are we for our departure from this world?

**3.** Look at the accounts of the transfiguration in the Gospels (Matt. 17:1–8, Mark 9:2–8 and Luke 9:28–36). Pick out the essential elements of the story. What stands out for you and challenges your faith?

**4.** If you'd like to study this idea further, the story in Exodus 33 concerns Moses meeting with God on the mountain and his reaction to that special time. Compare it to the transfiguration accounts and see if there are similarities or differences. What can you learn from this and how would you react to such an encounter?

**5.** Give people in the group these Bible passages to read aloud. Spend some time discussing how much the prophet delivering the message actually understood the message that they brought. Isaiah 7:3–16 may be particularly relevant here.

**6.** There is much debate as to whether prophecy is still evident in the church today. Often things that are brought to the church appear to be trivial and unhelpful. On the other hand, sometimes a seemingly insignificant prophetic picture opens up an issue that needs dealing with. We must treat prophetic words, pictures and dreams with care because God sometimes surprises us with His wisdom.

**7.** Teaching on the second coming of Christ is often in short supply in churches today. Discuss together its importance for your spiritual life and whether you are ready for His return. David Pawson's book *Explaining the Second Coming*[1] might be helpful.

**8.** Many of the false teachers that Peter was contending with at this time claimed to have mystical experiences that gave them special knowledge. How then do we judge the spiritual experiences that we sometimes have? Are we in danger of being led astray by an experience that cannot be grounded in Scripture? How can we protect ourselves from that danger? On the other hand, how do we make sure we do not miss something that really is from God?

[1]D. Pawson, *Explaining the Second Coming* (Lancaster: Sovereign World Ltd, 2002)

# Week 4: The Dangers of Deceptive Promises

## Opening Icebreaker

Do make sure that when you select some newspapers that they are suitable! They do not need to be from the same day. What you are looking for are stories that illustrate the problem of deception and lies in our world today. Concentrate not so much on the morality but on the damage that is caused to unsuspecting people. There may be some stories from your life when a con artist has taken you in. If you are able and if it is helpful, talk about how you felt at the time and any short/long-term effects that you have suffered because of it.

**Aim of the Session**

To be alerted to the dangers of false teachers in the Church and to be able to identify deceptive promises that are made by those seeking their own ends.

**Discussion Starters**

1.  We often have a problem with achieving the right tension between truth and grace. We need to be watchful and aware of the lies of false teaching whilst not slipping into the perils of being judgmental. It is very easy to point the finger at others when we may have missed the point of what they are saying. Discuss how we can get the balance right. If you have not received any teaching recently about cults and groups that deviate from the truth of the Bible, perhaps you could encourage your leaders to arrange a short course.

2.  Discuss what are the basic issues that define a cult – you might look at control, authority, ideas about God etc. It might also be useful to be sure about what you believe about God, Jesus, the Holy Spirit, the incarnation, death and resurrection. When you have the real thing you can spot a counterfeit!

3.  If God is so generous towards us, who have rebelled and gone our own way, then, if we are going to display a family likeness, we too should be open-handed. People in the group may have stories to share here of God's miraculous provision for them. What does true Christian giving look like in a world that is compassion fatigued? Perhaps discuss practical tips.

4.  When it comes to integrity a good question to ask ourselves is: 'What am I like when no one's looking?'

Think of some examples of integrity in the Bible and in your world. You might look at Joseph or Nehemiah. Perhaps discuss how accountability partners are important, especially for those in paid Christian ministry.

**5.** Look again at biblical leaders like Pharaoh, Herod, Solomon, David and tease out how they slipped up in this area. Ask the question of yourself too: 'Am I in danger of being seduced by power? The following quote by Lord Acton might be useful to discuss: 'Power tends to corrupt and absolute power corrupts absolutely.'[1]

**6.** The false teachers offered secret knowledge, unbridled sensual passion and the potential of financial advancement. Little wonder that some were taken in by their teaching! Try to discover what Peter says about their debased lifestyle in the letter. The Early Church dealt with this kind of behaviour rigorously but how will we handle people like this in our own church?

**7.** Look at Revelation 20:7–15 and discuss the issues surrounding future judgment. What will the judgment of God look like? What verses of Scripture will inform us as we work through this issue?

**8.** Do you have any examples of ways that God has delivered you in time of extreme danger or trial? Read 2 Corinthians 6:3–10, 11:16–33 for Paul's account of God's deliverances. Turn your discussion of experiences into thankful prayer.

[1]Lord Acton, *Historical Essays and Studies* (1907)

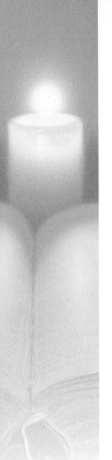

# Week 5: The Destiny of Promise Deceivers

## Opening Icebreaker

The point of the game is to show that some stories seem very plausible when they are told with sincerity. However, sincerity is not the only test we need to apply when we are seeking to find the truth.

## Aim of the Session

To understand and develop a pastoral response to those who are intent on perverting the truth of the gospel.

## Discussion Starters

**1.** It is very easy for us to become arrogant in our Christian lives. After all, we have as Christians an assurance of salvation and a promise of eternity with Jesus! But if we believe that we have complete knowledge then we are no better than the false teachers. We must always leave room for mystery or we are in danger of falling into the arrogance trap.

**2.** In their egotism, the false teachers of Peter's time felt they could slander and blaspheme against the angels. These teachers were so self-willed that they had no regard for civil or heavenly authority. Find a good description of blasphemy and discuss how we can handle this in our everyday lives when people around us indulge in this kind of speech.

**3.** Due to the fact that apostolic teaching had been distorted, the door was open for the false teachers to claim that anything went in terms of morality. It seems that even at love feasts and breaking of bread services, sexual temptation proved too much for some. We live in highly sexually charged times with unhelpful images displayed everywhere. What is our reaction as Christians and how do we manage to remain pure when beset with sexual temptation?

**4.** Travelling teachers in the first century could make a reasonable living out of the gifts from adoring followers. The false teachers exploited this and increasingly they operated out of a system of greed. Is greed a problem for us as we attempt to 'keep up with the Joneses'?

**5.** Freedom can mean many things for people today. What appears to be freedom can in fact actually be slavery and exploitation. Take some time to consider and pray for those who are still slaves in the sex industry or garment trade. What is true Christian freedom and are you living in the fullness of the freedom that Christ brings?

**6.** Consider the quote from Nelson Mandela, a man who had experienced imprisonment and the delight of release. Is it possible to be free ourselves and yet hold others in bondage by the way that we behave? How can you help others grow in their God-given freedom?

**7.** This is a very tricky subject that can generate plenty of heat but not a lot of light! It is very likely that the people that Peter referred to here were actually not members of God's family (see Week 5's Opening Our Eyes section). However, is it possible to become so apostatic that you turn your back on God, finally and completely, and are you still a Christian?

**8.** Leadership can be a lonely business and our leaders need all the support we can give them. What part can you play as a group in helping your leaders to keep growing and know that they are loved? Here are some possibilities: pray for them regularly, encourage them with an email or card, send an anonymous gift of chocolates, flowers or tickets to a special event.

## **Week 6:** The Promise of Christ's Return

### Opening Icebreaker

There will have been times for all of us when we faced some scepticism or scoffing from a variety of sources. Often we are at a loss as to how to reply and our response may be inadequate. Do some thinking about what are the usual objections and work out together how you could reply. It is not a case of winning an argument but sharing our love for Jesus effectively.

### Aim of the Session

To learn how to be an effective and proactive witness for Christ when faced by opposition.

### Discussion Starters

**1.** It is good to spend some time thinking back over how God has spoken into your life previously. Can you recall the challenge He brought and the response you made? This could have been through reading the Bible privately, through the preached Word or when a prophetic word had been brought to the church. Often we need to be reminded of these life-giving words.

**2.** Peter is eager to stimulate his friends to do some godly thinking. How can we help one another to review our thought patterns? The Greek word for 'wholesome' carries the meaning of being sifted until pure or being held up to the light to show how spotless it is.

**3.** When we are faced by opposition and criticism, do we seek to answer the question rather than digging a bit deeper to find what is at the root of the question? There may be some lingering hurt or wound that needs addressing before the issue raised is tackled.

**4.** There is always a challenge to spend more time with God's Word in spite of our busyness. If we are going to be effective witnesses for Christ we need to grow in our understanding of how to use and apply His Word to our daily lives. Discuss helpful tips for growing in this way (eg, sitting quietly and waiting to hear what God is saying though Scripture, using a Bible reading aid etc).

**5.** The second coming of Christ is a doctrine that is often forgotten in our regular teaching. Yet I wonder what difference it would make to our discipleship if we lived with the thought that 'it could be today'? Think about how it can stimulate your Christian walk and bring focus to life.

**6.** Revelation 21 is a great chapter full of anticipation of what is to be. Although we must live in the present, there is also a need to be living with a future hope. So, what are you looking forward to most? Meeting Jesus face to face, reuniting with loved ones; having a new body with no more pain or sickness?

**7.** In thinking about the return of Christ, Peter draws the attention of his friends to the fact that although the promise has not yet been fulfilled, they could have confidence in the promises of God. Read Psalm 90:4 and share about the importance of remembering that God inhabits eternity and is not bound by time. The false teachers had largely overlooked this concept.

**8.** The very good reason that Peter gives in answer to the sceptics, who questioned the timing of the second coming, is that God is patient and wants people who are far away from Him to have more time to respond

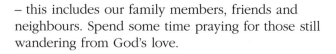

– this includes our family members, friends and neighbours. Spend some time praying for those still wandering from God's love.

## Week 7: Looking Forward

### Opening Icebreaker

This icebreaker allows the group to think about their dreams (and discuss them if they wish to), especially questioning whether their dreams, if fulfilled, would add to the kingdom.

### Aim of the Session

To challenge our thinking about our direction and purpose in life and encourage a diligent attitude in our daily walk with Christ.

### Discussion Starters

1.  I sometimes wonder whether the difference between a Christian and their unbelieving neighbour would be spotted from the outside. There is a clear call in these final verses to live a life that honours Christ and is markedly different to others.

2.  The words in Mark 13:10 infer that Christ will not return until the good news of the gospel has been shared with all nations. If that is the correct interpretation, then we have a strong motivation for sharing our faith. How are we playing our part in the great narrative of the salvation story?

3.  How different will the new heaven and earth be from the present one? Use your imagination but remember that God's thoughts are beyond our thoughts (Isa. 55:8).

**4.** Do you live with urgency, determined to be like Jesus? What are the signs that we have begun to coast and that other things are becoming more important? If you had only twenty-four hours to live, how would you spend them?

**5.** Think back over the story of the Old Testament and try to discover the times when God was patient with His people. Think about the Exodus wanderings, or the constant wanting to be like other nations with idols to worship. How has God showed patience with you? Share those moments and give Him thanks for His grace and love.

**6.** When Paul wrote to the Philippians, he wanted to address the lack of unity amongst them. So he calls them to be like-minded, have the same love and to be one in spirit and purpose (Phil. 2:2). How is it going in your church or group? Are you united in your love of God and devotion to His Son? What can you do to help your church or group to be one in spirit?

**7.** The warning to the church at Ephesus in Revelation 2 is just as relevant to the Church today. In being so sold out on seeking truth, we can forget how to love Jesus and by implication, each other. How can we help each other to be watchful but not always suspicious?

**8.** Spend some time encouraging one another with observations of how you have seen each other grow in the grace and knowledge of Jesus these last few months. What a joy it is to be able to encourage others and to be encouraged!

# Continue transforming your daily walk with God.

## Every Day with Jesus

With around half a million readers, this insightful devotional by Selwyn Hughes is one of the most popular daily Bible reading tools in the world. A large-print edition is also available.
72-page booklets, 120x170mm

## Life Every Day

Apply the Bible to life each day with these challenging life-application notes written by international speaker and well-known author Jeff Lucas.
64-page booklets, 120x170mm

## Inspiring Women Every Day

Written by women for women of all ages and from all walks of life. These notes will help to build faith and bring encouragement and inspiration to the lives and hearts of Christian women.
64-page booklets, 120x170mm

## Cover to Cover Every Day

Study one Old Testament and one New Testament book in depth with each issue, and a psalm every weekend. Covers every book of the Bible in five years.
64-page booklets, 120x170mm

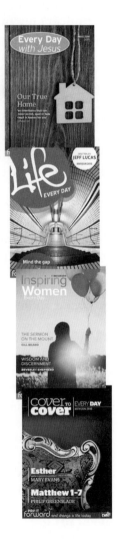

For current prices or to order, visit **www.cwr.org.uk/store**
Available online or from Christian bookshops.

# Journey through the Bible as it happened in a year of daily readings

Read through the entire Bible in a year with 366 daily readings from the New International Version (NIV) arranged in chronological order.

Beautiful charts, maps, illustrations and diagrams make the biblical background vivid, timelines enable you to track your progress, and a daily commentary helps you to apply what you read to your life.

A special website also provides character studies, insightful articles, photos of archaeological sites and much more for increased understanding and insight.

### *Cover to Cover Complete* - NIV Edition
1,600 pages, hardback with ribbon marker, 140x215mm
ISBN: 978-1-85345-804-0

# Latest resource

### Mary - The Mother of Jesus

Uncover timeless truths from what we know of Jesus' mother, Mary. How she reacted to the news that she would give birth to the Son of God, and how she lived and communicated during His time on earth, can teach us much about how God wants us to act today. Perhaps one of the most famous women of all time, whatever our denominational background, we can celebrate Mary's life and learn from both her struggles and her joys.

72-page booklet, 210x148mm
**ISBN: 978-1-78259-402-4**

# The bestselling *Cover to Cover* Bible Study Series

**1 Corinthians**
*Growing a Spirit-filled church*
ISBN: 978-1-85345-374-8

**2 Corinthians**
*Restoring harmony*
ISBN: 978-1-85345-551-3

**1 Peter**
*Good reasons for hope*
ISBN: 978-1-78259-088-0

**2 Peter**
*Living in the light of
God's promises*
ISBN: 978-1-78259-402-4

**1 Timothy**
*Healthy churches –
effective Christians*
ISBN: 978-1-85345-291-8

**23rd Psalm**
*The Lord is my shepherd*
ISBN: 978-1-85345-449-3

**2 Timothy and Titus**
*Vital Christianity*
ISBN: 978-1-85345-338-0

**Abraham**
*Adventures of faith*
ISBN: 978-1-78259-089-7

**Acts 1–12**
*Church on the move*
ISBN: 978-1-85345-574-2

**Acts 13–28**
*To the ends of the earth*
ISBN: 978-1-85345-592-6

**Barnabas**
*Son of encouragement*
ISBN: 978-1-85345-911-5

**Bible Genres**
*Hearing what the Bible really says*
ISBN: 978-1-85345-987-0

**Daniel**
*Living boldly for God*
ISBN: 978-1-85345-986-3

**Ecclesiastes**
*Hard questions and
spiritual answers*
ISBN: 978-1-85345-371-7

**Elijah**
*A man and his God*
ISBN: 978-1-85345-575-9

**Ephesians**
*Claiming your inheritance*
ISBN: 978-1-85345-229-1

**Esther**
*For such a time as this*
ISBN: 978-1-85345-511-7

**Fruit of the Spirit**
*Growing more like Jesus*
ISBN: 978-1-85345-375-5

**Galatians**
*Freedom in Christ*
ISBN: 978-1-85345-648-0

**Genesis 1–11**
*Foundations of reality*
ISBN: 978-1-85345-404-2

**God's Rescue Plan**
*Finding God's fingerprints
on human history*
ISBN: 978-1-85345-294-9

**Great Prayers of the Bible**
*Applying them to our lives today*
ISBN: 978-1-85345-253-6

**Hebrews**
*Jesus – simply the best*
ISBN: 978-1-85345-337-3

**Hosea**
*The love that never fails*
ISBN: 978-1-85345-290-1

**Isaiah 1–39**
Prophet to the nations
ISBN: 978-1-85345-510-0

**Isaiah 40–66**
Prophet of restoration
ISBN: 978-1-85345-550-6

**James**
Faith in action
ISBN: 978-1-85345-293-2

**Jeremiah**
The passionate prophet
ISBN: 978-1-85345-372-4

**John's Gospel**
Exploring the seven miraculous
signs
ISBN: 978-1-85345-295-6

**Joseph**
The power of forgiveness and
reconciliation
ISBN: 978-1-85345-252-9

**Judges 1–8**
The spiral of faith
ISBN: 978-1-85345-681-7

**Judges 9–21**
Learning to live God's way
ISBN: 978-1-85345-910-8

**Luke**
A prescription for living
ISBN: 978-1-78259-270-9

**Mark**
Life as it is meant to be lived
ISBN: 978-1-85345-233-8

**Mary**
The mother of Jesus
ISBN: 978-1-78259-402-4

**Moses**
Face to face with God
ISBN: 978-1-85345-336-6

**Names of God**
Exploring the depths of
God's character
ISBN: 978-1-85345-680-0

**Nehemiah**
Principles for life
ISBN: 978-1-85345-335-9

**Parables**
Communicating God on earth
ISBN: 978-1-85345-340-3

**Philemon**
From slavery to freedom
ISBN: 978-1-85345-453-0

**Philippians**
Living for the sake of the gospel
ISBN: 978-1-85345-421-9

**Prayers of Jesus**
Hearing His heartbeat
ISBN: 978-1-85345-647-3

**Proverbs**
Living a life of wisdom
ISBN: 978-1-85345-373-1

**Revelation 1–3**
Christ's call to the Church
ISBN: 978-1-85345-461-5

**Revelation 4–22**
The Lamb wins! Christ's final
victory
ISBN: 978-1-85345-411-0

**Rivers of Justice**
Responding to God's call to
righteousness today
ISBN: 978-1-85345-339-7

**Ruth**
Loving kindness in action
ISBN: 978-1-85345-231-4

**The Covenants**
God's promises and their
relevance today
ISBN: 978-1-85345-255-0

**The Creed**
Belief in action
ISBN: 978-1-78259-202-0

**The Divine Blueprint**
God's extraordinary power in
ordinary lives
ISBN: 978-1-85345-292-5

**The Holy Spirit**
Understanding and experiencing
Him
ISBN: 978-1-85345-254-3

**The Image of God**
His attributes and character
ISBN: 978-1-85345-228-4

**The Kingdom**
Studies from Matthew's Gospel
ISBN: 978-1-85345-251-2

**The Letter to the Colossians**
In Christ alone
ISBN: 978-1-85345-405-9

**The Letter to the Romans**
Good news for everyone
ISBN: 978-1-85345-250-5

**The Lord's Prayer**
Praying Jesus' way
ISBN: 978-1-85345-460-8

**The Prodigal Son**
Amazing grace
ISBN: 978-1-85345-412-7

**The Second Coming**
Living in the light of Jesus' return
ISBN: 978-1-85345-422-6

**The Sermon on the Mount**
Life within the new covenant
ISBN: 978-1-85345-370-0

**The Tabernacle**
Entering into God's presence
ISBN: 978-1-85345-230-7

**The Ten Commandments**
Living God's Way
ISBN: 978-1-85345-593-3

**The Uniqueness of our Faith**
What makes Christianity
distinctive?
ISBN: 978-1-85345-232-1

For current prices or to order, visit **www.cwr.org.uk/store**
Available online or from Christian bookshops.

# smallGroup central

### All of our small group ideas and resources in one place

# Online:

**www.smallgroupcentral.org.uk**
is an exciting new website filled with
free video teaching, free tools and a
whole host of ideas.

# On the road:

We provide a range of seminars
themed for small groups. If you
would like us to bring a seminar to
your local community, contact us at
**hello@smallgroupcentral.org.uk**

# In print:

We publish books, study guides and
DVDs covering an extensive list of
themes, Bible books and life issues.


Log on and find out more at:
**www.smallgroupcentral.org.uk**

# NATIONAL DISTRIBUTORS

**UK: (and countries not listed below)**
CWR, Waverley Abbey House, Waverley Lane, Farnham, Surrey GU9 8EP.
Tel: (01252) 784700 Outside UK (44) 1252 784700 Email: mail@cwr.org.uk

**AUSTRALIA:** KI Entertainment, Unit 21 317-321 Woodpark Road, Smithfield, New South Wales 2164 Tel: 1 800 850 777 Fax: 02 9604 3699 Email: sales@kientertainment.com.au

**CANADA:** David C Cook Distribution Canada, PO Box 98, 55 Woodslee Avenue, Paris, Ontario N3L 3E5  Tel: 1t800 263 2664 Email: joy.kearley@davidccook.ca

**GHANA:** Challenge Enterprises of Ghana, PO Box 5723, Accra  Tel: (021) 222437/223249 Fax: (021) 226227 Email: ceg@africaonline.com.gh

**HONG KONG:** Cross Communications Ltd, 11/F Ko's House, 577 Nathan Road, Kowloon Tel: 2780 1188 Fax: 2770 6229 Email: cross@crosshk.com

**INDIA:** Crystal Communications, Plot No. 125, Road No. 7, T.M.C, Mahendra Hills, East Marredpally, Secunderabad - 500026 Tel/Fax: (040) 27737145 Email: crystal_edwj@rediffmail.com

**KENYA:** Keswick Books and Gifts Ltd, PO Box 10242-00400, Nairobi Tel: (020) 2226047/312639 Email: sales.keswick@africaonline.co.ke

**MALAYSIA:** Canaanland Distributors Sdn Bhd, No. 25 Jalan PJU 1A/41B, NZX Commercial Centre, Ara Jaya, 47301 Petaling Jaya, Selangor Tel: (03) 7885 0540/1/2 Fax: (03) 7885 0545 Email: info@canaanland.com.my

Salvation Publishing & Distribution Sdn Bhd, 23 Jalan SS 2/64, 47300 Petaling Jaya, Selangor Tel: (03) 78766411/78766797 Fax: (03) 78757066/78756360 Email: info@ salvationbookcentre.com

**NEW ZEALAND:** KI Entertainment, Unit 21 317-321 Woodpark Road, Smithfield, New South Wales 2164, Australia  Tel: 0 800 850 777 Fax: +612 9604 3699 Email: sales@kientertainment.com.au

**NIGERIA:** FBFM, Helen Baugh House, 96 St Finbarr's College Road, Akoka, Lagos Tel: (+234) 01-7747429, 08075201777, 08186337699, 08154453905 Email: fbfm_1@yahoo.com

**PHILIPPINES:** OMF Literature Inc, 776 Boni Avenue, Mandaluyong City Tel: (02) 531 2183 Fax: (02) 531 1960 Email: gloadlaon@omflit.com

**SINGAPORE:** Alby Commercial Enterprises Pte Ltd, 95 Kallang Avenue #04-00, AIS Industrial Building, 339420 Tel: (+65) 629 27238 Fax: (+65) 629 27235 Email: marketing@alby.com.sg

**SOUTH AFRICA:** Life Media & Distribution, CNR Hans Schoeman & Rabie Streets, Randpark Ridge, RANDBURG 2056 Tel: (+27)0117964157 Fax: (+27)0117964017 Email: ennies@lifemedia.co.za

**SRI LANKA:** Christombu Publications (Pvt) Ltd, Bartleet House, 65 Braybrooke Place, Colombo 2 Tel: (+941) 2421073/2447665 Email: christombupublications@gmail.com

**USA:** David C Cook Distribution Canada, PO Box 98, 55 Woodslee Avenue, Paris, Ontario N3L 3E5, Canada Tel: 1800 263 2664 Email: joy.kearley@davidccook.ca

**CWR is a Registered Charity - Number 294387**
**CWR is a Limited Company registered in England - Registration Number 1990308**

Seminars and events

Waverley Abbey College

Publishing and media

Conference facilities

# Transforming lives

CWR's vision is to enable people to experience personal transformation through applying God's Word to their lives and relationships.
Our Bible-based training and resources help people around the world to:
• Grow in their walk with God
• Understand and apply Scripture to their lives
• Resource themselves and their church
• Develop pastoral care and counselling skills
• Train for leadership
• Strengthen relationships, marriage and family life and much more.
Our insightful writers provide daily Bible reading notes and other resources for all ages, and our experienced course designers and presenters have gained an international reputation for excellence and effectiveness.
CWR's Training and Conference Centres in Surrey and East Sussex, England, provide excellent facilities in idyllic settings – ideal for both learning and spiritual refreshment.

 **Applying God's Word**
*to everyday life and relationships*

CWR, Waverley Abbey House,
Waverley Lane, Farnham,
Surrey GU9 8EP, UK

Telephone: **+44 (0)1252 784700**
Email: **info@cwr.org.uk**
Website: **www.cwr.org.uk**

Registered Charity No. 294387
Company Registration No. 1990308